GOD AT WORK

In Times of Trouble

Text © 2000 by
Saint Meinrad Archabbey

Published by One Caring Place
Abbey Press
St. Meinrad, Indiana 47577

Library of Congress Catalog Number
00-101213

ISBN 0-87029-343-5

Printed in the United States of America

GOD AT WORK

In

Times
of Trouble

Edited by R. Philip Etienne

Abbey Press
St. Meinrad, Indiana 47577

Introduction

Trouble ... the word itself conjures up different things to different people. To some, it may suggest a physical malady—through illness, injury, or hazard. Others may regard *trouble* as a spiritual or emotional crisis. And others may include everyday hurdles that we all must negotiate. Sometimes the meaning varies by what's currently affecting or threatening an individual ... today's emergency might be little more than an afterthought tomorrow.

But there's one thing about *Trouble* that's almost always true: if you have someone to help you with a problem, it's easier to tackle it. When we share our concerns with a loved one or close friend, the burden is lightened. And no matter what the challenge is, monumental or mildly trivial, we should always consider God as our greatest friend.

God at Work … in Times of Trouble consistently reflects that theme through the many stories that follow. Through recollections of harrowing close calls, spiritual crises, and emotional issues, we see, time after time, that God loves us and cares for us and about us. God knows that we all need help sometimes; and whether we find it through the actions of others, through a strength found inside ourselves, or through an unexplained, miraculous event, we can take heart that it was inspired from above.

God at work ... it's a reassuring concept, isn't it?

—R. Philip Etienne

Trust in the Lord with all your heart, And lean not on your own understanding; In all your ways acknowledge Him, And he shall direct your paths.

—Proverbs 3:5-6

Blessing in Rush Hour

By Janet A. Sullivan

It was in the fall of 1990. As precious metals investment advisors, three associates and myself drove northbound out of Manhattan in late afternoon rush hour traffic. We had just attended a two-day seminar sponsored by the World Gold Council and now, homebound, we began the 240-mile road trip back to Portsmouth, New Hampshire.

It was raining moderately and the sun had not quite set. Our dependable Bill commanded the wheel of his sleek, black Saab 9000. Jean, his close friend since high school, accompanied him in the passenger's seat, while I sat in the back with Marion, who was eight months pregnant, to my right.

Hurried vehicles surrounded us as we traveled in the second of four jammed lanes leaving the city. After several minutes of stop and go, the traffic sped up to about 35 m.p.h., at which time I thought, "Okay, now we're on our way!"

Grateful to be a passenger and not the driver, I let my mind and body settle into a passive posture and watched the bustling rhythm of the city from a comfortable distance. To our left, a small concrete wall divided us from the anxious inbound vehicles, and I was happy not to be in one of them. Musing out the right window, beyond Marion's placid profile, I viewed teaming traffic jutting out from beneath us and rushing toward a maze, already overloaded with cars, trucks, and vans all anxious to get to their destinations.

Suddenly, I was jolted out of my relaxed state and realized that our vehicle was swerving on the wet surface, assuming a haphazard S-swerving motion. Tension immediately replaced repose as we were helplessly turned in dizzying 360-degree spins. Bill was not in control of the wheel.

Taking what action she could, Jean shouted a string of directions, each with increasing urgency: "Take your foot off the brake! Foot off the brake! Bill! Take your foot off the brake!! Off the brake!!" Marion and I sat stunned and mute, far from the controls of the front seat. Instinctively, I extended my right arm across Marion's protruding belly to protect and to prevent her and her unborn baby from thrusting forward.

Reeling as if we were on a carnival ride, the car increased in momentum each time it swooped around and around. I saw a concrete wall coming at us at least three times; yet, there was never an impact. What looked like was going to happen each time we spun, just didn't happen.

Then, everything inside and outside the car became slow-motioned, and I felt a blanket of silence envelop us. It felt as though we were cushioned, protected. An incredible and unmistakable sense of serenity overtook me and I had

the impression that the very prop-
erties of time and space had
changed. I felt, right then, that we
were in the hands of something
very powerful, something eminently
blessed. I didn't know what the out-
come for us would be, but I did
know with all certainty that what-
ever was going to happen, it would
be okay. We were in God's hands.
We were literally in God's hands.

Rather than jolting to a stop, or
slamming into the concrete abut-
ments, our car came to a gentle rest,
as if we were carefully placed there.
We were, however, faced sideways in
the center of the expressway, just
beyond a bend in the road. Our car
was a sitting duck, obstructing two
lanes; and if hit, we would be
broadsided on Bill's and my side.

I turned my head to the left and glanced out my window at the road we'd just traveled, before the car had gone into what seemed like minutes of disarray. To my great astonishment there was no traffic in sight! None. But I was still aware that when the lanes of vehicles would begin to come forward, they would not be able to see us until practically right up on us. And with the slick, rainy road conditions, successful braking would be difficult.

Bill sat inert, in shock at the driver's wheel, while Jean and Marion sat silent. I could actually feel a cushion of love and gentleness surround us and fill the space of the car. I felt without a doubt the assurance that we were going to be okay—but we had to act!

Seeing that we were all unhurt, I found myself calmly delivering quick instructions to Bill. My voice was level and without panic, "Bill, we are okay. There are no cars. Just put the car in reverse, back up and swing straight ahead. There are no cars, Bill, and we are okay. Just go ahead and drive normally. When the cars come, they are going to wait for us. We are going to be all right. The cars will wait for us, Bill. They will wait."

I could feel Bill responding and, with gentle ease, he put the car in reverse as I watched traffic approach from around the bend. In a strange, silent rhythm—like a precisely orchestrated symphony—each first car, with a string of ready vehicles in tow, gradually came into view and glided to a stop about eight feet from where our car sat broadside.

Lane by lane they came to attention in a seemingly rehearsed fashion; their movement orderly, even compliant, and completely unlike random, hurried traffic. I watched in quiet amazement. Bill continued his efforts to correct the direction of the Saab and I continued to calmly assure, "The cars are waiting, Bill. They are waiting. You are doing great."

Here, in the midst of New York City rush hour traffic, there wasn't a single honk from an irate horn. Bill successfully righted the car's direction and slowly drove ahead. It seemed to me, then, that time speeded back up. City noise flooded my senses and our vehicle was once again smothered within the midst of a thick swarm of unrelenting traffic.

During the whole ordeal, it was as though we had been frozen in time. Then, when it was over, it seemed we'd been fast-forwarded to the next sequence of events. Like we had experienced a glitch in time and were given another chance. None of us spoke.

Not far ahead were rows of toll booths which led out of the city. A wide-eyed attendant stuck his neck out to glance at each of us while Bill, with uncharacteristic confusion, dug from pocket to pocket for unready toll money. "Unbelievable! You people are very lucky! Very lucky!" said the man.

"Yeah," muttered a still-shocked Bill, just before driving on.

Excitedly, I blurted out, "We've just experienced an intervention. We have just experienced a Divine Intervention!" Never in my life had I uttered those words. They just came to me as I knew, without question, that we had been involved in something miraculous.

For about five or more minutes, we drove in silence. Then, simultaneously, we burst into vigorous chatter about the incident, excitedly exchanging our perceptions of what had just occurred. For the remaining four-and-a-half-hour trip home, we rode in a comfortable and musing silence with one another—each lost in our own thoughts ... each, I'm sure, extremely grateful for what didn't happen to us ... and each completely awed and grateful for what did.

The next morning, when I arrived at the office and saw no one around, I followed the sound of excited voices coming from the boss's office. Bill, Jean, and Marion were gathered there, replaying our unbelievable and blessed experience from the afternoon before.

As I entered the spirited room, Marion energetically turned to me and said, "Oh, Janet! We were just telling Bob! Tell him ..." I joined in and we stood about detailing and deciphering—the amazement of it all still clearly with each one of us. That was the highlight of our trip ... What gold seminar? What meeting? We had experienced a golden meeting with God!

After a bit, we broke up our discussion to find out what the precious metals had done overnight in Tokyo, and thus to thankfully begin a new day.

In thinking back, it was as though the great and loving hands of God had come out of the sky and parted the seas ... in this case, the traffic ... and placed us ever-so-gently out of harm's way. A most magnificent and memorable event, the grace of this heavenly experience will never leave me.

How do I define a Divine Intervention? Simply put, it is an experience whereby we recognize, in the moment, the loving hand of God touching us, blessing us, and protecting us. And by the Lord's loving and gentle, yet awesome, power, we feel unmistakably, and with great humility, the amazing hand of God at work in our lives.

*C*onsult not your fears but your hopes and your dreams. Think not about your frustrations, but about your unfulfilled potential. Concern yourself not with what you tried and failed in, but with what it is still possible for you to do.

—Pope John XXIII

When God Stepped In

By Ruth C. Webb

Forty years ago, an event occurred that confirmed my belief in God. I was depressed and angry because I could not get a job utilizing my college degree. I was living at home with my parents, who left me alone during the day while they were at work. I had few friends and could not join social activities because cerebral palsy often made me so tense that my unsteady gait caused me to fall, and unclear speech made it difficult for strangers to understand me.

I was lonely and cried much of the time when I was alone. I began to recall the many times people had rejected me because they did not understand I was a human being in spite of my sometimes hard to understand speech and my distracting movements.

My loneliness made me long for a job where I could support myself and help others. I wanted to use the counseling techniques I had learned in college; I knew if I had the opportunity to counsel, I would succeed in helping people.

I had tried to seek employment from the Federal Office of Vocational Rehabilitation in Washington, D.C., and had been severely rejected by an agent. He could not look beyond my handicaps and told me that my dream of helping others was an impossible one.

The week after this interview, I was alone one afternoon and began to cry. I don't know how long I was weeping in my powder room when suddenly my apartment door opened and I heard Father Joe's voice asking: "What is the matter, Peggy? Why are you crying?" Father Joe was the pastor of our church, a tall man with a deep voice who lived one house down from us.

I was quite surprised to see him, since he usually didn't stop by our house on his homeward journey. "Why are you here?" I inquired. "How did you know I was crying?"

He came into the powder room and put his arm around me. "I was walking by your house when I felt the urge to turn into your driveway and come up your ramp," he answered. "What's the matter?"

"Nobody wants me. I can't get a job. My degree is useless," I cried. "I am no good."

Father Joe lifted my chin and peered directly into my eyes. "You are a child of God, and he doesn't make useless children. You may have to hunt for a job a little harder than most people, but I'm sure that God has a plan for your life," he assured me. "It may be that in your search you'll learn something that will help you when you do find the right job. Don't give up."

"I think that we each have lessons to learn while we seek the purpose for our lives," he explained.

"You have only just begun to look. You have your life before you, and I am sure you will find God's purpose for your life."

"I have a thought," he continued. "Next Thursday evening, the well-known author and healer, Agnes Sanford, is coming to our church. Would you like to come with your parents to hear her?"

I had met her the previous year, when she came to the Women's Association meeting. I had asked her then if she could heal me, and she said she couldn't do a thing for cerebral palsy. But I decided that I would enjoy hearing her again.

After Mrs. Sanford's sermon, my dear dad went up to her and invited her to talk to me. He did not know of my previous conversation with Mrs. Sanford. She agreed to meet with me, but as she was walking down the aisle towards me, something frightening happened: I began to scream "No! No! Don't come near me!"

I suddenly became two people: an actor and an observer. The observer was horrified by the actions of the actor, but she couldn't get the actor to stop screaming. Suddenly, I became aware that Father Joe was entering the church door. He walked quickly up to me, and I began to cry. He put his hand on my shoulder and said: "Don't cry now. You can do that later."

He then looked me in the eye and said, "Peggy, I think I know what you want to do. You want to talk to Mrs. Sanford alone."

I answered, "Will you be there?"

He nodded and walked over to Agnes. After directing her to his office and telling my parents that he would take me home, he escorted me to his study where Agnes was waiting by the window.

Agnes spoke quietly: "There was a time when I couldn't go near a window without wanting to jump out and commit suicide. God healed me of that impulse and gave me the power to heal others. Do you want me to pray for you?"

Through tears, I sobbed, "Yes."

Father Joe knelt in front of me and Agnes put her hand on my head and asked God to take the impulse for suicide away from me. A warm feeling, like a cup of warm soup, flowed into the top of my head and down through my whole body. The desire to end my life was gone and did not trouble me again for a long time. I felt light and happy. After thanking Agnes, Father Joe took me home.

The next morning, I drove the two blocks to Father Joe's study in my motorized wheelchair. He told me about the amazing summons he had received in his office across the street the night before. He said, "I sat down to write my sermon when I had an impulse to get up, put on my coat and come over to the church. I didn't know what I was supposed to do until I saw you, screaming and crying."

"You said just the right thing to make me stop crying," I said. "How did you know?"

Father Joe looked at me tenderly and said, "Peggy, we were all in the hands of God last night."

That night was a turning point in my life. I could no longer doubt that God was with me and was guiding my life. Although I have been depressed many times, the memory of that night always fills me with awe and affirms once again that God is with me, no matter what the circumstances.

*B*etter than a thousand useless words is one single word that gives peace.

—Dhammapada

A Shirt Full of God's Tears

By Jim Auer

He was waiting in the hall outside my classroom right before dismissal, a student of three years ago, barely holding back tears in spite of the bustle of younger students around him. The pain of something gone terribly wrong cried out silently from his face.

That didn't surprise me. I knew him well, although we hadn't been in frequent contact recently. Many things had gone wrong in his life. Some had simply happened to him—a broken family, bleeding relationships. More recently, the problems were of his own doing, and I knew about them, usually by his own admission.

The journey downward had begun with occasional marijuana use, escalated and branched into other substance abuse, and branched still further into more arenas of what a psychologist would call self-destructive behavior, or perhaps simply bad decisions. A theologian would call it the effects of original sin.

The terms don't matter all that much when you're confronted with a suffering 17-year-old who has just seen his world blown up by his own hand: the police bust, the expulsion from school, the disgrace to family, the destruction of plans for a bright future both athletically and scholastically, the drab anticipation of drug rehab, the daunting prospect of picking up the pieces and starting all over again.

When the hallway and my classroom had cleared, we sat across from each other ... very briefly. Then he leaned toward me, and I held him through heaving sobs and barely audible or recognizable words. Only our Maytag washing machine could have drenched my shirt more. He stayed on my shoulder for easily 15 minutes, not moving even when, twice, a kid came into the classroom to retrieve a left-behind textbook.

And then we talked. I can't remember 10 exact words of what I said, but I remember the message: how good he was beneath the debris of his life, that God loved him, that I loved him.

It happened at a time when I was doubting what I heard a priest say at a retreat my wife and I attended: "You are indispensable to God's plan." It was beginning to seem like a classic warm fuzzy phrase; I was having a difficult time feeling even somewhat needed, much less indispensable. But perhaps I was that afternoon; and so perhaps I am still.

It was, after all, my classroom he sought and my shirt he soaked. No hero story, there; I just fumbled through it, praying silently for the right words.

God sent me a hurting kid. Or, more theologically, God came to me hurting and needing. And God, being God, makes good choices.

Whenever I start to doubt myself—which is frequently—I think of that. I still have trouble with "indispensable;" but "important" feels right.

What lies behind us and what lies before us are small matters compared to what lies within us.

— Ralph Waldo Emerson

Removing the Blinders

By Fr. Joe Weigman

When I was a kid, I loved to watch the parades that were held downtown. I loved the clowns, the bands, the horses. I always felt sorry for the horses, though. It seemed cruel to me that they had to wear blinders that blocked their vision. The blinders, of course, were necessary to prevent the horses from being startled; but I suppose I was afraid that the horses would not be able to see well enough to make the journey through the twists and turns of our downtown.

Today, as an adult, I still feel bad about blinders—not the ones that horses wear but the ones that we all wear from time to time. Yes, regrettably, I sometimes wear blinders, but I have also experienced the grace of taking them off to gain perspective. In the process, I have learned more about what God's vision must be like.

I was in the physical therapy area of a hospital. While my therapist left for a moment, I sat down and could not help but overhear the conversation between another therapist and another patient. The patient was a woman about 75 years old. As they sat down together to my left, the physical therapist suggested to the woman that she might consider beginning to use a cane. "Oh, no," the woman exclaimed, "I could never do *that*."

When I heard the protest, I felt myself becoming resentful and a little arrogant. "Hmph," I thought to myself, "how dare you get so upset about using a cane. Here I am, using a forearm crutch and a cane, and I am less than half your age!" I wished I could be as lucky as her, where my disability would be the result of advanced years and not the multiple sclerosis diagnosed near the beginning of my young adulthood.

While I sat there, becoming absorbed in self-pity because of the situation to my left, a new situation presented itself to my right. There was a little boy, probably four years old, nearing me as his therapist traveled behind him. The boy used two forearm crutches, and was held upright with the therapist's harness. From the looks of things, he could have been as resentful of me as I was of the older woman next to me on the other side. Instead, the little boy was laughing, and then he stopped in front of me to say hello and to tell me his name. He appeared to be having the time of his life.

As Darren continued on his way, I was reminded in a very vivid way: yes, I have it worse than some, but not as bad as others. There, in the physical therapy area of the hospital, I realized that I sometimes have trouble seeing beyond my own struggles and challenges; in other words, I sometimes wear horse blinders. I felt then and there that I was being called to broaden my vision by removing them. The call, I believe, came from God.

Just as I feel called to remove the blinders that occasionally prevent me from seeing beyond myself, so too are we all called by God to broaden our perspective. God's world is big, after all. When our perspective broadens, we become better able to see ourselves and others the way God sees all of us: broken in our own ways, but worthy of love and compassion. We also become better able to see our way through the twists and turns of life's journey that we travel together.

*N*ot I—not anyone else
can travel that road for you,
You must travel it for yourself.
                    —Walt Whitman

Right in My Own Back Yard

By Lorri Malone

"Dear Lord, just get me outta this town!" Moments of utter frustration were often laced with that phrase ... as were moments of sincere prayer.

I had lived in my tiny hometown my entire life and I had longed to move on to a larger city. There, I imagined endless opportunity, culture, diversity, and shopping. Those were things missing from my hometown and they were things I desperately desired.

I got my wish when I was hired by a corporation and asked to relocate to a large metropolitan area. My husband, Kevin, and I sold our house, went house hunting in our new community, plunged into his job search, and prepared for the birth of our first child. We were overwhelmed, but nonetheless excited.

Things fell into place rather seamlessly. We bought a brand-new house in a pleasant neighborhood and Kevin landed the job he wanted. My prayers, apparently, were finally answered.

Once we were both settled into our new jobs and our home, it wasn't long until our son arrived. During my maternity leave, I found myself rather lonely and homesick. My job had turned out to be much more challenging than I had anticipated, and I felt insecure leaving it unattended during maternity leave.

Our new home, while very nice, lacked the character and space of our former home. The new neighborhood seemed less pleasant and more stark, since the surrounding homes were either under construction or newly constructed and vacant. I missed my family. I missed my friends.

I began to question if relocating had been the right decision. I wondered if we should just pack up and go back home.

"We wouldn't be here if God didn't want us here," I would remind myself half-heartedly. "The way things fell into place for us was no coincidence."

But my reasoning fell into the old watch-what-you-ask-for-you-just-might-get-it lesson. Perhaps I was just homesick or perhaps God was trying to teach me the virtues of my previous existence. I prayed to know what God's plan was for us. Should we stay or should we go back to where we came from? "Lord, let me know the right thing to do and I'll do it," I promised.

A few days later, Kevin and I were in our back yard with the baby, surveying the lack of grass, which was common among the new houses. Kevin pointed out a woman in the yard adjoining ours. She, too, was checking out patches of brown grass in her yard.

"I noticed a 'Sold' sign out front of that house last week," he said. "I'll bet she's our new neighbor. Let's go introduce ourselves."

As we approached, the woman looked up and smiled at us. "Oh," she said. "You have a little baby! How old?"

"He's two months old, almost three ..."

"Ohmigod," she interrupted, as a look of shock washed over her. "Lorri, you don't recognize me, do you?"

Totally perplexed, I took a couple of steps closer and really looked her in the face. Her name popped into my head and right out of my mouth at the same time.

"Missy! Is that you ... you bought this house?"

She was nodding frantically. Downright giddy, we were both practically jumping up and down with excitement. Had I not been holding a snoozing infant in my arms, I would have jumped our gate in sheer hysteria. Missy and I had been hometown friends since elementary school and had chummed around in high school. After graduation, we lost touch; but I still thought very fondly of her.

And now she was my neighbor—along with her husband (who was also from our hometown) and five-year-old daughter. My loneliness came to an end when they moved in next door. Our husbands play golf together. Missy and I take the kids shopping. We go out to dinner together. We talk across the fence during the afternoon and on the phone at night.

My prayers for a new job, home, and lifestyle had been answered. I was blessed with a loving husband and a beautiful son. And when I still questioned if I were worthy of all these blessings, God gave me the answer ... and it was right in my own back yard.

We are healed of a suffering only by experiencing it to the full.

—Marcel Proust

A Story of Forgiveness and Growth

By Angie Garrett

The day that would change my life forever was just an ordinary day up to the point when I received a telephone call.

I had just arrived at home from my job and I was starting to prepare dinner for my family. My day had been very hectic and demanding at work and the anxiety and stress of the day was starting to become visible. The phone rang and I silently said to myself, "Please don't let it be for me."

It was my Aunt Bertha from back home in southern Indiana. She was my Dad's older sister and I had always enjoyed a close relationship with her—in fact, she was my favorite aunt.

"How are you?" she asked. I responded with a cheerful hello and answered that I was fine. I knew instantly that something was wrong because she sounded depressed. She proceeded to inform me that my dad, whom I had not seen in almost 20 years, was very ill and she thought I should give him a call.

My dad was a full-fledged alcoholic and had made drinking a way of life—a life which did not include his family. He was an abusive alcoholic who had put his wife and four children through a life of chaos and torment in the 17 years he had been around.

He had deserted his family when my younger sister was only two years old. He took off for parts unknown and eventually ended up in Florida. He would occasionally track me down and call when he was drunk, and would try to borrow money (to buy more alcohol, I am sure). He would always give some lame excuse as to what he needed the money for at the time, but I always saw straight through his lies.

It had been a blessing in disguise, a real "Work of God," when he did leave us, because it probably saved our lives. Dad was so violent when he was drunk that he did horrible things to his family and had "black-outs," not remembering the next day what he had done until he saw the terrible destruction before him.

He used to load up his old rusty shotgun and sit in his big easy chair daring anyone to confront him. In the meantime, my mother would sneak her children out the back door, one at a time, to a safe hiding place. When Dad realized we were all gone, he would start cursing and threatened to shoot anyone that moved. I remember him shooting at my mother once, as she was running down a country road; but because he was so drunk and it was dark, thankfully, he missed!

So as you can already figure out, I had no respect or love for my Dad. He changed our lives forever, forcing us to grow up in that volatile and terrorized atmosphere. Only those of us who have been there can really understand what that kind of life is really like. I used to pray for my dad all the time when I was growing up. Sometimes I would pray for him to just quit drinking and other times I would pray for him to just die!

Still, somewhere inside of me was a quiet and hidden compassion for him. And sometimes these feelings came through. He was such a lonely, desolate man—lost within himself with no real direction or purpose in his life.

And now, while talking on the phone with my aunt, I realized that God was at work within me. I could feel a quiet calm about myself that had never been there before. Usually, when my dad's name was mentioned, I became very nervous and upset. But now I found myself promising my aunt that I would call Dad and see what was going on.

After dinner, I made the phone call, as I promised I would, and spoke with my dad for the first time in many years. He was very weak and gravely ill; and he did not sound like the drunken, abusive man that had been etched vividly in my mind for all those years.

My dad, it turned out, had terminal lung cancer. He asked me to come see him, and to bring him to my home to live until his death. I only had 24 hours to make a decision that would have a huge impact on not only myself, but my family as well. I really had to do a lot of soul searching and praying to God for guidance in this decision. I kept asking God, "Why is this happening? I don't know if I can handle seeing my dad—especially because of all the anger I have felt towards him for so many years."

I realize that God may not always reveal His reasons to us, but I also feel that everything happens for a specific reason. This was an extremely difficult time for me: my husband was away from work, recovering from major brain surgery and I didn't feel I had any strength left to deal with another crisis.

I prayed into the night and asked God to give me the strength to make the right decision—the one I knew God wanted me to make.

I realized that God puts us through many tests of our faith in our journey through life. And I had to believe that I could trust God's plans for me at this time. I was on the plane that evening to visit my dad and bring him back with me.

It was a very emotional reunion and I will never forget the sad, lonely look in Dad's eyes when I walked into that hospital room. He was sitting in a wheel chair, staring down at the floor. I touched him on the shoulder and said, "Dad, it's me." He looked up and wasn't completely sure who I was.

He finally asked, "Is it really you?" Then he started to cry and very humbly said, "I didn't think you would really come."

I told him that I had come because I knew God wanted me to do this, so I could learn to forgive him. We could learn to be a family again, or at least try, in the short time that God had given us together.

My dad lived just about a year after coming to stay with me. But in that brief time, we shared together and I learned to forgive him for all the things he had done because of his drinking. I came to learn how alcoholism had the power to rob not only the body but the mind and spirit of the person afflicted.

I was able to seek counseling for myself, to learn how being a child growing up in an alcoholic abusive home also had affected my adult life. I feel that final year with my dad was in God's plan all along and it was through God's grace and mercy that I became a much better person.

I was able to let go of all the anger I had kept inside of me for so many years; and I came to realize that my Dad was just a man, like any other man, who had his faults and human frailties. I know now he did not intentionally plan to hurt his family, but was overcome by a force far more powerful than he could resist.

Being able to forgive my dad and have some quality family time with him before he died has left me with the peace for which I had always been searching. I know now that being able to forgive someone, no matter what they've done, is definitely a sign of "God At Work."

Grant, Lord, that we might overcome our enemies by transforming them into friends. Make them and make us conscious of those deep inward reaches whereby every heart is rooted in our world's deep common life.

—Jewish Prayer

A Thorn in My Side

By Mildred Tengbom

I was discouraged—thoroughly discouraged, frustrated, and disillusioned! I always had prided myself on being able to get along with people. Now I was coming to the horrible realization that I could not get along with others—more specifically, with one person in particular.

When I assumed a position as secretary in a large urban church, the minister suggested that perhaps I would like to share an apartment with the parish visitor, whom I will call Linda.

The arrangements were made. The parish visitor was a woman 10 years my senior: a very lovely person, friendly and gracious. But for some reason, things she did began to irritate me like a hangnail.

Linda liked to stay up late; I liked to get up early. I couldn't get up early if I got to bed late. Furthermore, when she stayed up late, she liked to spend a couple of hours reading in bed. But we shared a bedroom. Try as I might, I could not ignore her reading light. So even if I retired at a reasonable time, I could not get to sleep.

Linda was neat in every other way, but she had the habit of leaving her shoes and slippers lying around. It irritated me to no end when I stumbled over them. My irritation finally became so great that when I tripped over one of her shoes, I would savagely kick it, sending it flying across the room.

When I was working, Linda often used the phone in my office. Her conversations were quite lengthy, as people discussed their problems with her. If I continued my typing, she couldn't hear her conversation on the phone. So there I would sit—helpless, idle, work stacking up—while I waited for her to get off the phone and on with her visitation.

I was a bit overweight, and Linda never let me forget it. Every time we sat down to a meal, she would faithfully total up my calories. It got so bad that one day, when we were eating banana cream pie, I was tempted to throw my pie in her face.

Our relationship got worse and worse until even my work efficiency was affected. I began having trouble sleeping at night. I became thoroughly distressed by the ugly picture of myself which was developing—a Christian worker not being able to get along with another Christian!

I became so disillusioned that I could no longer bring myself to attend staff prayer meetings. I felt I already was hypocrite enough. Why add to my hypocrisy by praying piously in front of others?

This was the state of affairs until one particular Thursday. I had awakened early and had been unable to get back to sleep. So I arose, showered, dressed, and walked to the church. At least I could be alone there, completely alone, before the phone began to ring. Maybe in the quiet of my office I would be able to sort out my thoughts.

I rested my head on my arms at my desk, and almost unconsciously began to pray. It was a very free manner of praying ... I just began to talk things out with God.

"I'm miserable," I confided, "utterly miserable! I hate myself! And how you must hate me ... to think that I am stumbling on a little thing like this."

Minutes passed. I was mute.

"God, I have tried and it just will not work. I'm all worn out." Silence again.

Then I added, "But I feel so bad about it, Father. I know this isn't the way you want things to be." Pause. More thought.

"Father, I give up. I'm sorry, but I just can't love her."

Though I hurt all over, even tears wouldn't flow to help relieve my tension. I felt cold and empty and numb inside. What in the world had I done? Where was God anyway? Had he left me completely? Was this why I felt like I did?

"Father, I don't know what else to do but turn the whole miserable mess over to you. Will you take it? Can you forgive me?" Pause. I knew God could. I knew God would.

I didn't feel forgiven. But feel it or not, I would act as though I was, because I knew Scripture states clearly that God will always forgive the contrite.

"Father, I want you to take over completely. I want you to move right into my heart and being. I want you to love this person through me. I can't. But I believe that you do. And I ask you to do it through me."

Linda didn't show up in the office at all that morning. When I walked home at noon to join her for lunch, I prayed all the way, "Lord, take over now. Love her through me. You do it. You do it."

When I saw her, I was amazed to discover that the old feelings of resentment didn't flare up.

"Wonderful, Father," I exulted. "Wonderful. But you keep things under control. I'm weak. You must love her through me."

I had to maintain this minute-by-minute dependence on God whenever I was with her. By the end of the week, Linda said to me, "I don't know what has come over you!"

"What do you mean?" I queried.

"All of a sudden, you've become so nice to me!" she explained.

I turned around quickly, so she wouldn't see my grin. "Father," I whispered in my heart, "it works! It really works!"

As the weeks and months passed, our friendship deepened. And to this day, I'm glad for the moment when I turned to God and exclaimed, "I give up!"

*L*ife can only be under-
stood backwards, but must be
lived forwards.

—Soren Kierkegaard

Learning Why

By Carol Luebering

I taught the neighbors' girls to
sew, listened to their frustrations,
encouraged them in their interests. I
danced at their weddings, proud of
the dresses they had made with my
help. I thought of them as my
"other daughters." And I didn't
know why.

The women, whose knitting
problems I untangled in a needle-
work shop, surprised me by confid-
ing their deepest sorrows. I could
sense pain beneath the words of
rude customers and discovered that,
with a little patience, I could draw it
out. And I didn't know why.

My parish discerned a need to
provide care for people in crisis.

Delivering meals seemed a natural for me; but, instead, I signed up for the bereavement committee. I found a home there, and was soon writing about our experience. And I didn't know why.

At the publishing company where I later went to work, I acquired more "other daughters"— the young women on the staff. I thought I knew why: my age made me the perfect confidante and mentor. But I didn't really know why.

Ten years ago, my phone rang. A young woman with pain in her voice tried to explain why she was calling. "I think you knew me as an infant," she told me, but her name meant nothing to me. Finally she got it out: "I think I'm your daughter." Soon I was embracing a young woman I had given up for adoption when I was 18.

With the joy I felt at meeting her at last came waves of the pain. I relived the sorrow I had sealed away for many years. Bearing a child out of wedlock in those years was a matter of great shame, a secret never to be mentioned. You were supposed to sign the release, forget all about the stranger you had carried, and get on with your life.

Now I know why my life unfolded as it did. Under God's guiding hand, I was traveling a long road to healing. And now I know that the best parts of me are formed, thanks to God's grace, from scar tissue.

*F*aith is to believe what we do not see; the reward of this faith is to see what we believe.

—Saint Augustine

Spirit in Bloom

By Nancy Stout

In early spring of this year, I made my annual trek to the Abbey of Gethsemani for a week of retreat. This year, driving up to that marvelous Cistercian monastery in Kentucky was a particularly emotional arrival for me. I suppose I feared I might not return this year because of the relentless health struggles I've been facing. But, I made it!

As usual, I sunk right into the familiarity of the place—the rhythm of life there that is like no other place I know. I was delighted to see the faces of the monks in the choir; I feel as if they are all my friends. And to know they have been there, each and every day, at prayer and at work, is such a powerful realization for me.

I brought to retreat a heavy issue I've confronted and worked with in spiritual direction in recent months, and I hoped to hear God speaking to me, guiding me on how to handle this issue. What would the message be?

I walked to the top of the hill to sit by the statues depicting Jesus in the Garden of Gethsemane along with the sleeping disciples. After spending some meditative time there, just pondering things, I started back down on the woods path. Along the way is a tiny prayer hut with a bench, prayer cards, rosaries, and journals in which to write.

I looked up my entry of last year in the journal book. Then I started writing of how it was for me now, and I wrote a lot. After 15 minutes or so, I walked out of the prayer hut to continue my walk, and I was suddenly aware of how much better I felt! It was a dramatic change in mood; the restlessness I came with was eased, my spirits were lifted, and there was a sense of inner peace and calm that had eluded me for some time. What happened in that prayer hut? Who else was there with me as I prayed?

I can only conclude that I was touched by the Holy Spirit—that God was present there with me, bestowing God's grace on me to help me move forward in a journey where I was stuck. And then I saw it on the pathway at my feet: a lone purple crocus in full bloom! And it occurred to me that the flower dared to bloom, to open itself, right on the path where it might be trampled or, worse yet, not noticed at all. It bloomed as a sign of God's gifts of beauty in this world.

I knew in that brief moment of wonder that I would be okay—I will be okay. Even if things do not go well for me in terms of my health struggle, I will still be okay! And the Lord wishes me to continue to bloom, to dare to open myself to God's love, God's presence, and God's direction in my life. I am not alone like the crocus; I have many people around me who care and love and support me. And the Lord walks with me, helping me to shoulder my cross, even carrying me along when things are hardest. I must dare to bloom also!

Had I left the Abbey that very day, I would have felt the retreat was complete. I entered seeking the quiet in which I could hear God above the other noise of everyday life. I listened hard, and the voice came, in a tiny wooden prayer hut, in the woods of Kentucky—and in the beauty of that single purple crocus.

God at Work Series

- *God at Work…
  in Times of Loss.* #20096

- *God at Work…
  in Times of Trouble.* #20095

- *God at Work…
  Through the Voices of
  Children.* #20097

Available at your favorite bookstore
or gift shop, or directly from:
One Caring Place, Abbey Press,
St. Meinrad, IN 47577
(800) 325-2511
www.onecaringplace.com